Orisons

Soulful Reflections

Kim P. Sami

Orisons - Soulful Reflections
First published by Kim P. Sami 2021
Copyright © Kim P. Sami
Illustrations © Dee Copeland

The moral right of the author has been asserted.
All rights reserved. Without limiting the rights under copyright reserved above, no part of this publication may be reproduced, stored in or introduced into a retrieval system, or transmitted, in any form or by any means (electronic, mechanical, photocopying, recording or otherwise), without prior written permission.
For permission contact the publisher at kimpsami@gmail.com

This book is sold subject to the condition that it shall not, by way of trade or otherwise, be lent, resold, hired out, or otherwise circulated without the publisher's prior consent in any form of binding or cover other than that in which it is published and without a similar condition including this condition being imposed on the subsequent purchaser.

A catalogue record for this book is available from the National Library of Australia

Cover and internal design by Barbie Robinson –
Writing with Light
https://writingwithlight.com.au/
Cover image and internal illustrations –
Dee Copeland
https://deeartwork.com/dee-copeland/

First edition printed in Australia by south*west* printing
Unit 3/50 Topham Road
Smeaton Grange NSW 2567 Australia
https://www.southwestprinting.com.au/

Orisons – Soulful Reflections
ISBN 978-0-909497-64-4 paperback

For Augustine (Gus) Sami, my husband,
my teacher, mentor and friend, Mauro Di Nicola,
my counsellors,
and all those who have helped me sing my life-song

AUTHOR'S INTRODUCTION

An Orison is a prayer or plea to a deity. This comes from a Latin word meaning to speak, and it means to speak to God (https://www.vocabulary.com>orison).

My first way of expressing myself was through music and lyrics, literally giving voice to the deep emotions and thoughts inside me. Hymns and songs said what I couldn't find the words to say and fed that spark of life within me. As a young adult, I started journalling, finding my own words to try and sort out my thoughts and feelings, particularly regarding the opposite sex. Mum was also having problems coping with her youngest child exerting more independence, which led to considerable conflict between us.

My journalling inevitably turned into prayer, as I sought help from the One who had kept that spark of life in me and helped me navigate my path. Other people, such as Mauro Di Nicola (author of the Foreword) offered support when life was becoming too difficult – then, and now. I have also been fortunate in gaining good counselling over years, as I grapple with life's problems, grief and pain (past and present).

One day, the 'stream of consciousness' way of expressing myself in my journalling became more poetic, and suddenly I found myself using poems to give voice to what was on and in my heart.

This volume of poems (my first) is a sample of the many I have written from around 1992 up to the present. They speak and reflect on past pain, the struggle to free myself from life-denying ways and what helps me to do so, to live a life that is abundant, fulfilling, meaningful.

Although I try and use words instead of 'God' in my poetry to express that life within me, I invite you to use any other expression or word/phrase that resonates with you. Whatever it is that fills you with peace, gives your life meaning, feeds that spark within you. My hope is that you may find something in these poems of mine that may assist you in your own life's journey and give you hope for today and the future.

FOREWORD

I have known Kim Sami for over 40 years, initially as her English and General Studies teacher in senior high school and as something of a mentor in more recent times. For as long as I have known her, Kim has evinced and embodied an unswerving passion for life combined with a profound dynamic desire to explore it in all its contours and often jagged particularity. This is clearly evident in all that she writes, and particularly in her poetry. Kim's passion for life and for the dignity and truthfulness of both her suffering and her joys, are among the many gems that readers will find in *Orisons*.

Kim's poetry and songs began as very personal 'stream of consciousness' searches in her private journal, sketches in different poetic forms of both inner exploration and outer experience. Over time what became increasingly evident was that what had initially been intensely personal, private and at times tentative explorations, were becoming 'publishable'.

As Kim grew in her capacity to see and hear and value herself, her poetry became increasingly able to be shared with others who had not known her personally. Over time, the journey inward and the journey outward became increasingly a single journey able to be articulated poetically as if in counterpoint. The result is *Orisons*, a beautiful and graceful collection of poems with, not surprisingly for someone with as great a love for music and song as Kim, something of the lyrical quality of psalms.

Similarly to the psalms, Kim's poetry is not afraid to confront and voice intense experiences of suffering, rejection, dejection, hurt and grief. Particularly poignant in this collection is *To be Seen*, with its intense desire to be seen and accepted by those closest to her 'just maybe, someday'. But who or what is to be seen is not the same as that which is merely visible, since 'Just as the cover of a book is not its story/So mine is not me' as pithily insisted in *Define Me*. No, the desire is for the 'real me' to be found, 'The one that was lost, and is being found' (*Refuge*).

Loss of control over life and meaning is articulated poignantly in *Vortex*, a powerful lament which uses rhythm and metaphor with insight and skill to evoke a sense of profound desolation. The stark confronting metaphors in this poem's line, 'Spat out and left for dead', are evocative of the poetry of T.S. Eliot. As a reply to perhaps well-intentioned consolation, *To Hold On* is a delightful example of the power of rhythm and cadence. As a fitting finish to this foreword, a recommendation not to miss *To the Younger Freer Me*, Kim's enchanting ode to childhood, and to the child in all of us, that is so reminiscent of Les Murray's *Spring Hail*, with Kim rejoicing in 'Breaking free, breaking out, no reason left for doubt'.

Mauro Di Nicola
October 2021

11 For I know the plans I have for you, declares the LORD, plans to prosper you and not to harm you, plans to give you hope and a future. 12 Then you will call on me and come and pray to me, and I will listen to you. 13 You will seek me and find me when you seek me with all your heart.

Jeremiah 29: 11-13 (NIV)
www.Biblegateway.com

MAKE THIS LIFE

Make this life of mine a *life*,
A life worth the name,
A life worth living.
Teach me what Jesus knew
the gentle art of living
in joy, in peace, in love
for you, Creator God,
for self,
for all of creation.

May such a life be lived each day
with tears
and laughter
with gentleness
and compassion
a life beyond measure
and peace without end.

May boredom be banished forever.
May curiosity grow.
May life be ever an adventure.
Be enjoyed, rather than endured.
Lived, rather than survived.
Cherished, rather than meaningless
An endless journey of discovery
with God as our constant guide.

FIVE YEARS OLD

Five years old, terrified
keeping all the pain inside
Five years old, full of fears
Choking back the heartfelt tears
An extremely aware and sensitive soul
Emotionally intelligent at five years' old
Bright as a button and full of life
but made to hide herself from sight

Unprepared for life at school
Compelled to conform to a regimented rule
Bullied and yelled at, made to feel small
Physically sick, couldn't cope with it all

They didn't know just what they did
they didn't mean to put the lid
on the Spirit of Life, that gave her the spark,
The joy in her eyes that lit up the dark.
How could they know how to treat one as she,
When they'd never been shown, were unable to see?

But now all has changed, healing is here
Those who hurt her, repent, and now see crystal – clear
They see her, they hear her, and send her their love
So this sad five-year-old can now fly like a dove

May this five-year-old now teach her much older self
the freedom of being the joy deeply felt
Of God's Spirit within her, no longer to hide
The person she always was, deep inside.

TO BE SEEN

The parents were blind, the brothers were, too
The sisters were likewise
What could she do?
The only sighted person in a world of the blind
Wondering if she'd go out of her mind
She saw a world of colours
Of richness, and of depth
Majesty of mountains, causing her to catch breath

How to explain to the blind ones she loved
The colour of rainbows
The flight of a dove?
How to describe what it's like to see
When blindness had been
their sole reality?

Seems foolish to try
To describe what she knew
But she tried, and she tried
'til her face turned blue
For she longed for them to understand more
The world that she lived in
The world that she saw
That she was no monster because she could see
In a world where blindness
Was what most seemed to be

For if they could see
Just some of the place,
The world that she lived in
Then they might 'see' her face
They might understand her and help her to grow

Be open to the wonder
That she'd come to know

But…

How can a person born blind ever see?
Or even imagine
What being sighted could mean?
If no surgery could fix it, then it's pointless to try
It's like teaching a bird without wings to fly
Why keep hitting your head
Against such a brick wall
When the only result
Is your head being sore?

The hope that, just maybe, someday they will see
That a miracle happens
And they'll really see me
For the person I am, and accept me for that
Not the image, the illusion
Silhouetted in black
I'll no longer feel different
But feel I belong
And joyfully, lovingly
Join them in song

DEFINE ME

Define me not by my appearance
By my hair, weight, skin
Tattooed or not,
Brown, pale, black, yellow,
Red from the sun
Or wrinkled with age.
Define me not by my possessions –
House, car, jewellery, clothes,
Expensive or cheap, fake or real.

Define me not by my career –
Lowly, high-flyer, white collar or blue,
Process worker,
Unemployed,
Cleaner, executive
Stay-at-home Mum.

Define me not by what I know –
Degreed, Diploma-ed,
Drop-out, self-taught.
A graduate of the school of hard knocks.

Define me not by my past,
Things you may have heard
That I've done, or not done
Or things that've been done to me

Define me, rather, by the words I speak,
The values I hold,
The way I treat you, and others.
Generous or not,
Self-serving or other-caring.

My actions, and the reasons for them
Speak far more clearly
And are far wider reaching
Than the superficiality
Of that which is readily seen.

Just as the cover of a book is not its story
So, mine is not me
Delve into the interior and spend the time,
It takes to truly know and understand me.
I may surprise you.

Then, and only then,
if you must,
Define who I am.

THE VOICE

There's a voice that's deep inside of me
It lives inside my head
At times, it's just a whisper
Sometimes, it would raise the dead
An insidious voice, persistent
Playing its own lying game
Perpetually in the background,
With a message that's always the same

It tells me I'm not good enough,
That none could ever love me
It hisses my talents are worthless
Too damaged to ever be free
It tries to suck all life from me
And leads me to despair
Convinces me that when I call
No one will ever be there

But Lord, despite that lying voice
Somehow your Spirit comes through
Lighting my way through the darkness
Leading me gently to you
You have made me in your image
Uniquely, one of a kind
You know me and love me, despite all my doubts
In your love, it's the real me I find

Begone, you sad, dark, lying voice!
Begone! I heed you no more!
The Spirit's song has replaced you in me
Now hear me, watch me soar!

NO!

There's a word that I am learning that I haven't used enough
It's a word that needs to be voiced everyday
It's a small word, not a tall word, has great power when it's used
To keep the draining energy away

I will say NO to the boss, I will say NO with a toss
Of my head to show I mean it, come what may
I will say NO to the Dean, I will say NO to the Queen
And no longer let myself be led astray

I will say NO to my friend, I will say NO 'til the end
Of my passive ways, so I will be set free.
I will say NO to my job, I will say NO to a mob
To allow the Spirit of Life to work in me.

TIME OUT

Time to start again, Lord
Time to start anew
Time to take a different track
to see a different view

Time to take stock
to stop, to think
Time to stop reacting
To feelings that make me sink.

Time to take some time out
Of the spiral that I'm in,
Time to find an exit
From this dizzy, panicky spin.

Time to re-evaluate
This thing I call my life
Time to grieve for what I've lost
To stop myself twisting the knife

It's time I took good care
Of Kim, this person, me
Time to stop harmonising
To work on my own melody.

It's time to break the cycle
Of behaviour I have learnt
Time to leap into adventure
Even if I get burnt.

Time to take a risk, I think
Time to risk being me
Time to trust that you, my Lord
will be where you've promised you'd be.

I NEED TO GO WITHIN AWHILE
(The original version of this poem is also published in the Canberra Christian Writers' Anthology 2021)

I need to go within awhile, so please, don't be offended
If, while I go within awhile, your needs are unattended
I need to tend my inner self, where the true me resides
I'm needing some quiet solitude, to recharge, and revive

This is not a selfish act, I care, and love you still
But unless I go within awhile, I fear I'll come to ill.
I need to let God's Spirit blow away and clear
The clutter and the debris of the lies that feed my fear

So, pray for me, while I am gone, that God will help me grow
And let the Holy Spirit always gently flow
The blessings of the Spirit, be open to receive
So I may come back to myself, never more to leave.

EVENING PRAYER

Don't want to think, to write, to pray
Don't want to relive what I did today
Just want to lie here, just want to sleep
To curl up in bed, on my back, off my feet

Too tired to think, to write, to read
Don't even know what to do but breathe
And lie here, relaxing in my bed
Providing some break for this dizzy head.

Bring peace to my soul this night, Lord, I pray
And bless all the efforts I made this day
Bless all my clients, relations, and friends
And keep all in safety 'til it's daylight again.

DARING TO DARE

Sailing high above fluffy white clouds, in a sky of brilliant blue
While I knew where I was going, not sure what I was going to
He'd answered my ad in a Christian magazine, but I'd not seen him yet
We'd emailed, written and phoned – he'd had to leave before we met
Thinking of a romance – long-distance – not at all
Yet here I was, in a silver-winged plane, flying to his door

My Dad said I was crazy, that I couldn't afford the flight
You know almost nothing about him, he said, so how could he be Mr Right?
I have to go, I told him, though I know I am taking a chance,
This stranger from across the sea might lead to my wedding dance

Fiji? Maybe Dad was right! Why on earth have I travelled?
And as I passed through customs my confidence unravelled
In the arrival hall I wondered whether he'd actually be there
But he smiled, he waved, he called my name, then gently stroked my hair

And so, it began, with this Indo-Fijian man, and a woman from Down Under
Under tropical skies with such love in our eyes, would this be a holiday wonder?
Well, what would you say, if I told you today, we made it well beyond there
Eighteen years on and we're still going strong –
You'll never know what you'll find 'til you dare!

REVISITING ME

No longer 5, no longer 10
Time to revisit the me I was then
The me I was when I was born
Before all the ridicule, the sadness, the scorn
Learning what was missing back then
When I was 5, when I was 10

When 5, when 10, when 20 plus
I missed out learning oh, so much
Low confidence, low self esteem
A tender-hearted one, that could not glean
How could I learn, how could I grow,
From those who, themselves, had yet to know?

Creative and bright, craving the light
The light of the Spirit, that burnt in the night
Sometimes so dimly, I could hardly believe
That the 'still, small voice' still existed in me

Not one I knew to help me grow
To nurture the seeds within me, or know
How to encourage, or even to see
The emotionally intelligent, shy and scared me

The adult me, now, is able to see
To hear, soothe, and love the much younger me
I can take her hand, and her tender heart
Love her uniqueness, lead her out of the dark
From the condemnation she's lived under so long
Encourage her to sing out loudly and strong
No longer to fear, be courageous and true
Live the truth of the Spirit her whole life through.

MY LITTLE ONES

My little ones aren't dead at all.
They live on in my heart.
They're with me every day and night
And death could not us part.

I couldn't hold them in my arms
In a world not theirs to share.
But they'll always be a part of me
And they know how much I care.

PEACE!

Peace!
Such peacefulness
coursing through me
With each breath, each heartbeat
It becomes deeper
Travelling through my body
Permeating every cell

If I can let it
The Peacefulness may just erase
The pain in my heart
Swamp it, change it
Devour it, banish it forever from my being
Until all that exists
Is Peace.

BETWIXT AND BETWEEN

Betwixt and Between, hormones are raging
Betwixt and Between, not adult, not child
Betwixt and Between, body fast changing
Betwixt and Between, emotions run wild

Betwixt and Between, hormones see-sawing
Betwixt and Between, no children any more
Betwixt and Between, time is now racing
Betwixt and Between, now what is life for?

Wait and see what I will do, good things are on their way
Wait and see what I will do, Evil won't have the last say
Wait and see what I will do, I will provide all
Wait and see what I will do, I will not let you fall.

You will win this battle,
I'm fighting hard for you.
You will always have everything you need
I am here to see you through.

TO THE YOUNGER, FREER ME

There is so much stimulation, I am bursting at the seams
Don't know just what to do or where to stand.
I am restless, with thoughts racing at a hundred miles an hour,
Flying high, without a place to land.

There's so much running through me now, I'm feeling like a kite
A great wind gust has jerked free from the string.
Swooping here, darting there, singing, laughing without care,
Hurtling skyward at the mercy of the wind.

Breaking free, breaking out, no reason left for doubt,
No shackles now, no chains can keep me bound.
Something's settled, deep inside, which cannot be denied,
A gentle, calming peace it seems, at last, I've found.

The Spirit of the One, the Creator of my song
Is bursting through the walls I've kept inside.
It is sacred, it is true, and pointing me anew
To the younger, freer me, who now can't hide.

FREEDOM

Freedom
flying high above it all
unfettered
free of restraints
that would keep
one tied to the ground.

Freedom to choose,
where no choice is wrong
And the only reason
To discard a choice
Is that it's life-denying.

Fear has no place
in a free life

Freedom
to go where the spirit blows
with no hesitation
to discern the direction

Freedom
is not money
is not power
is not status.

Freedom
is peace of mind
is being comfortable
with oneself
with the world.

Freedom
is fun
is love
is God,
For, without God,
there is no freedom
only bondage.

Freedom
is being truly alive.

SOMETIMES

Sometimes I wonder, and sometimes freak out
Sometimes I question what life's all about
Sometimes I'm anxious, and can't go to sleep
Sometimes I've had it and am out on my feet.

Sometimes I'm happy, sometimes in despair
Sometimes I wonder if anyone cares
Sometimes I'm running from here to there
Sometimes my energy dissolves in the air.

Sometimes I can't seem to find any light
Darkness enfolds me, there is only night
Sometimes I doubt I can ever be free
Of all the chains that stop me being me

Amid all the doubting, confusion, and pain
I feel your presence, Lord, and it lights me again
Lights up the hope that I someday may be
More than just sometimes; more ever, with Thee.

12 I know what it is to be in need, and I know what it is to have plenty. I have learned the secret of being content in any and every situation, whether well fed or hungry, whether living in plenty or in want. 13 I can do all this through him who gives me strength.

Philippians 4: 12-13 (NIV)
www.Biblegateway.com

REFUGE

I sat before my window in the golden light of afternoon
The sun shining on leaves of tall, proud gums,
My little refuge among the chaos swirling all around.
Alone, I found some peace, the time and space to be,
Breathe, think.

Talking aloud to the One
The only One who knew me completely, intimately,
Who kept the flame of life alive
When darkness would prevail.

I sit now at my desk, in my own place,
Shared with the one you chose for me,
Still needing time alone to think, to breathe.
No chaos without,
Except the virus and what the world creates.

This chaos is within,
Heart , mind, and soul.
I need music
Lyrics and melodies that echo,
My innermost thoughts, feelings
The language of my soul,
Soothing, illuminating.

Time and peace to come back to myself,
Find the real me.
The one that was lost, and is being found,
Is discovering, rediscovering, being discovered.
Writing, singing, talking out loud
To the One, and ones who care
To clarify, to mirror, to reassure.

The Spirit acts through everything –
Through sunshine, rain, Nature,
Silence, music, art
People, places, puppies
Books, tea,
And through authentic conversations.

Warm, soft blankets,
Rocking chairs,
Creativity in all its forms
Give life meaning
When love is at its centre,
And in the centre of me.

THE LIGHT GIVER
(Original version published in the 2020 Poetry Marathon Anthology)

In a deep, dark tunnel I found myself
The proverbial canary in the mineshaft
From a place of light above ground
That had become gradually greyer,
Darker, and more menacing
Day by day

There was a heavy, crushing weight on me
That pinned me to the ground
Pressing continuously on me
Making every breath a battle
Of mind and heart and my badly bruised spirit

It was a pit of despairing
A cold, wet, lonely place
Where I thought no-one could, or would
Come looking for me,
Let alone seek to rescue me

A light shone, dimly at first,
From an unknown source
Just as I felt I could hold on no longer
It seemed to come from the tunnel before me
Until it was dazzling
Brightness sparkled off diamonds embedded in the rocks
And I gasped with awe
as the weight that had held me down
Seemed to disappear

The light was the One
Who brought warmth
For my shaking, numbed body,
My mind, and heart
Infusing me with the joy of loving,
of caring, of gentleness.
Until at last I could rejoice
In the awesomeness of life.

THE SPIRIT OF CHRISTMAS

They say that the Spirit of Christmas
Is not so alight this year
With power bills skyrocketing
Few lights have appeared
Haven't heard of solar?
That's what we're using outside
It is costing us nothing at all now
To keep the Spirit alive

The sun is a free source of power
Beaming joyously from above
Heralding the birth of our Saviour,
Given to us out of love
The Son of God, the Light of the World
Which is what we are all called to be
The One who created the sun and the stars
Became human, like you, like me

Solar stars don't shine as brightly
As the one that was said to have shone
Over the place where Jesus lay
As the Angels sang their song
They are still a small reminder
Of the Love God has for us, free
The Love that forgives, heals, redeems
If we only have eyes to see.

CREATOR OF SONG

You, Creator God,
Are the Creator of the Song
Which You sing for all to hear
Sometimes we lose the melody
Make up variations of our own
Out of tune with Yours
Hearing only the discord we have created

You sent your Son
To lead the choir with the sweetest voice of love
And all above and through our noise,
The Song is heard once more
So, all who follow him
Can join again
In unison, sing in harmony,
The Song of Truth

IN MY ROOM

My room is filled to bursting
with so many precious things
Things I love that make me smile
And help make my heart sing.

I have my solar figures,
They dance, and nod and sway
My craft things for creating,
reminding me to play
My memories live there also
photos, cards, and such
Of my parents, friends, and family,
of all whom I love so much

My life is in a bookcase,
and in a set of drawers
Writings of my past days,
of closed and open doors
The tears, the joys, the triumphs,
imperfect thoughts, and dreams
Live on in every volume
of my journals' pages' themes

Gifts to give to others,
wait patiently on shelves
Books of heartfelt wisdom,
into their depths I delve
And the thing that brings me close,
to the One who dwells within
Is my precious music,
the songs I love to sing.

The songs that speak of my Saviour,
my Guide, my Love, my Friend
That express my innermost yearnings,
for love that has no end
The echoes of the past Me,
the songs that speak to me still,
Fill my room with the that peaceful Presence,
and renew my spirit, my will

I can be myself completely there,
no need to hide or pretend
My thoughts and feelings can fly there,
beyond the walls, with no end
My room is my sanctuary,
a place to feel, renew
The essence of Me resides there,
ideas and dreams to pursue.

Pictures and words remind me
of the Lord of my life, God's love
For me, here on earth, they lead me
to my heavenly home, above.

VORTEX

Caught inside a vortex,
Spinning round and round.
Caught inside a vortex,
Feet can't touch the ground.
Spinning faster and faster, now,
Caught inside its web.
Spiralling out of control, now
Spat out and left for dead.

Totally spent, totally done,
Left lying on the ground.
No compassion: 'Well, that's a shame!
A defective one, no one's to blame.
There's plenty more where she came from!
Line up, line up, and join the throng!
Join the Toxic Vortex Game!
You'll never, ever, be the same!'

Almost a year since I fell off.
Almost a year since I screamed out STOP!
Still parts broken, deep within,
From that dizzy, deathly, poisonous spin.
Time to allow the Spirit to mend
Renewing, new growth in me to tend
Providing room to thrive and grow,
With loving compassion, mercy, to show.

MADE OF MUSIC
'Thank you for the music, For giving it to me' (*Thank you for the Music* – ABBA)

I think in lyrics, in rhymes, in tunes.
My head is filled with song,
Not just once, or twice, a day
But each day, all day long.

Sometimes, a word just sets it off
Or a thought, a phrase, a strain,
A random song might come along
And lodge inside my brain

When it began, I do not know –
Sometime when I was young.
Music and song have always been
My refuge, joy and fun.

It's like I'm made of music,
It flows all though my veins
I can't imagine a world without song
To melt away the pains.

It is what I am made for:
To sing out, loud and clear
Whatever's in this heart of mine
For anyone to hear.

My heart and soul are in the songs
That reflect what I'm about
Praise to my God, the Creator of Song
Whose Spirit I can't live without

A DIFFERENT WAY TO BE

Living to a different rhythm
Living to a different rhyme
Living to a different tempo
Transcending usual space and time.

Living a gentler, kinder life
Living in peace, without, within
Stopping to enjoy the roses
Floating freely with the wind.

Flying, soaring, adventure awaits
Anticipation taking flight
Allowing wonder to overtake
Fear falters badly in its light

Author of Life, allowed to reign,
Slowly guides me how to be,
Illuminates the darkest night,
Leads the way to a liberated me.

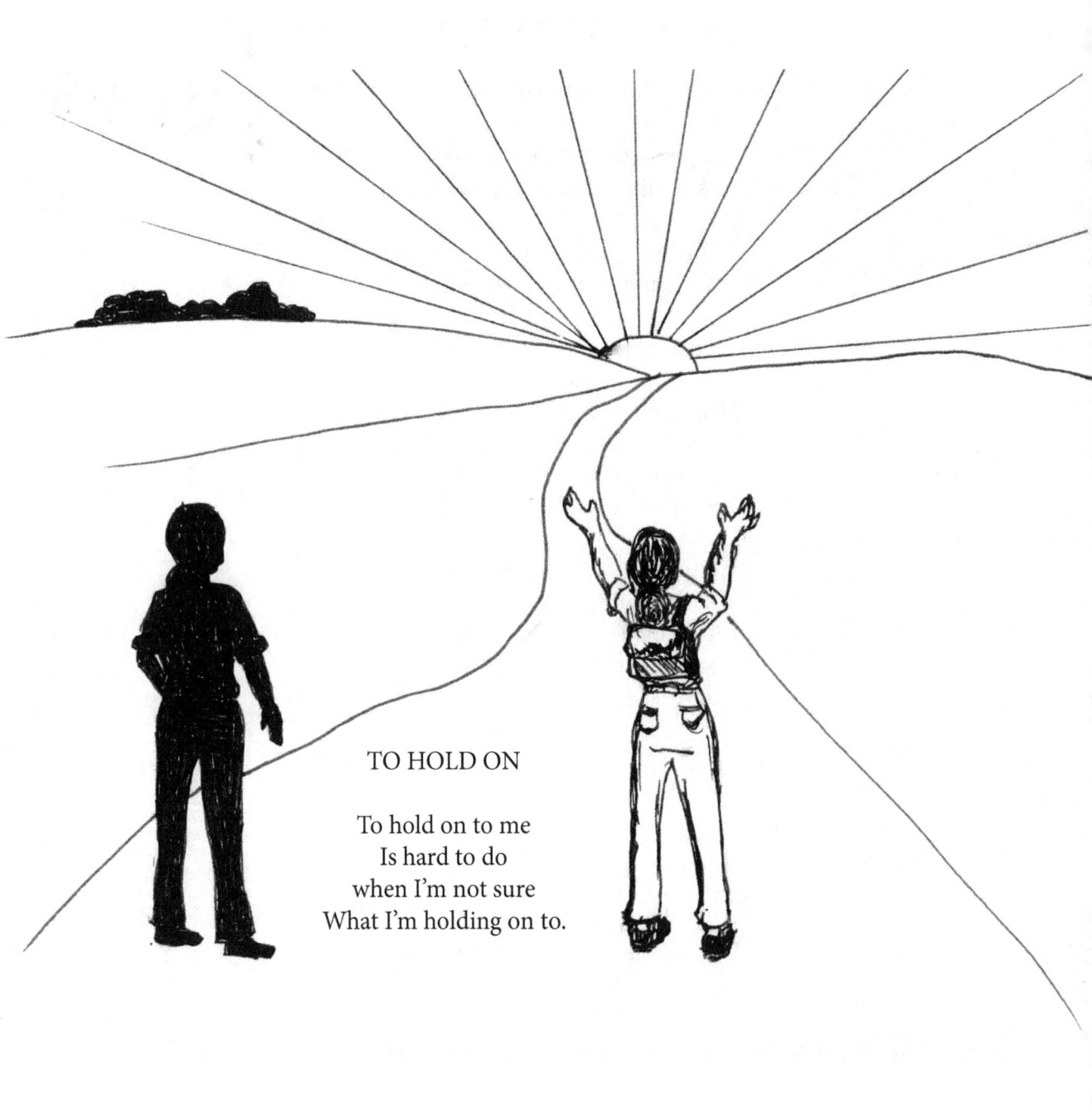

7 But we have this treasure in jars of clay to show that this all-surpassing power is from God and not from us. 8 We are hard pressed on every side, but not crushed; perplexed, but not in despair; 9 persecuted, but not abandoned; struck down, but not destroyed.

2 Corinthians 4: 7-9 (NIV)
www.Biblegateway.com

LEAP OF FAITH

It's all about that leap of faith
To fall into the unknown
Knowing that the Lord of Life
Is already there before us.

We fall, and like the eagle,
we're lifted on its wings
Love calls us forth,
Beyond the shadow of yesterday
Into the adventure of today,
With the strength to face each hour
Regardless of what may come.
Our arms embracing the future,
While we stay grounded in today
With the lessons and knowledge
Learnt from the seeds of the past.

FALLING INTO THE FUTURE

Needing to reauthor the story of my life
To see it all in colour, not greys, black or white
I need a different way to be
A different point of view
A different atmospheric vibe
One more infused by You

I cannot live as I once did
I need to change the scene.
Need to let more brightness in
Write a more enlivened theme.
Looking up, instead of down,
Slowing down the pace
Embrace all possibilities
With courage and faith, to face.

'You're already falling,
The one that is calling,
Is you.'

(From the song *The Voice* – by The Moody Blues)

LIFE-GIVING THINGS

Steaming hot showers on freezing cold mornings
Refreshing cool breezes on hot summer dawnings
The feeling of silky dog fur on my skin
These are a few of my life-giving things

Beautiful sunsets o'er peaceful still waters
Calming chai lattes with time just to loiter
When singing my heart out's like soaring on wings
God-given, wonderful, life-giving things

Breakfast in bed when there's no need to hurry
Days when there's blue sky and no need to worry
The warmth of the bright sun caressing my skin
These are some more of my life-giving things

Sitting alone still in soul-stretching dusk-times
Chatting to friends while we're hunting for cheap 'finds'
Yummy High Teas and a good chocolate binge
Just a few more of those life-giving things

Knitting and crochet and taking good pictures
Good conversations that leave me in stitches
Deep-felt connections that make my soul sing
Some more examples of life-giving things

Shopping for presents, unusual jewellery
New thoughts and music that sends thrills right though me
Engrossed in a good book and the worlds that it brings
More of those wonderful, life-giving things

When I'm hurting when life's painful
God can seem far away.
If I can partake of these life-giving things
God's love will come and stay.

The colour of blue in sky, sea, and cloth
The lush greens of tall trees in forests aloft
The perfume of roses, the coming of Spring
Add to the list of my life-giving things

The smell of fresh cut grass and freshly baked bread
The taste of fresh seafood and a stomach well-fed!
Days when I don't need to do anything
More of my lovely life-giving things

Sharing a kiss and a hug with my hubby
When he's focussed on me and not wrapped up in worry
His arm wrapped around me while out visiting
Is near to the top of my life-giving things

Feeling God's presence when singing His praises
Peace overcoming the dark, painful places
The contentment and happiness true love can bring
Is right at the top of my life-giving things.

ENLIGHTENED

Like rays of sunshine
fighting their way
through a murky, thick fog,
so your love
fights against the wall of lies
I once believed.
It penetrates my heart
To stay there
For ever more.

LIST OF WORKS AND FIRST LINES	PAGE
MAKE THIS LIFE Make this life of mine *a life*	1
FIVE YEARS OLD Five years old, terrified	2
TO BE SEEN The parents were blind, the brothers were, too	4
DEFINE ME Define me not by my appearance	6
THE VOICE There's a voice that's deep inside of me	8
NO! There's a word that I am learning that I haven't used enough	9
TIME OUT Time to start again, Lord	10
I NEED TO GO WITHIN A WHILE I need to go within awhile, so please, don't be offended	12
EVENING PRAYER Don't want to think, to write, to pray	13
DARING TO DARE Sailing high above fluffy white clouds, in a sky of brilliant blue	14
REVISITING ME No longer 5, no longer 10	15
MY LITTLE ONES My little ones aren't dead at all.	16
PEACE! Peace!	18
BETWIXT AND BETWEEN Betwixt and Between, hormones are raging	19
TO THE YOUNGER FREER ME There is so much stimulation, I am bursting at the seams	20

LIST OF WORKS AND FIRST LINES	PAGE
FREEDOM	22
Freedom	
SOMETIMES	24
Sometimes I wonder, and sometimes freak out	
REFUGE	26
I sat before my window in the golden light of afternoon	
THE LIGHT GIVER	28
In a deep, dark tunnel I found myself	
THE SPIRIT OF CHRISTMAS	30
They say that the Spirit of Christmas	
CREATOR OF SONG	31
You, Creator God,	
IN MY ROOM	34
My room is filled to bursting	
VORTEX	36
Caught inside a vortex,	
MADE OF MUSIC	38
I think in lyrics, in rhymes, in tunes.	
A DIFFERENT WAY TO BE	39
Living to a different rhythm	
TO HOLD ON	40
To hold on to me	
LEAP OF FAITH	42
It's all about that leap of faith	
FALLING INTO THE FUTURE	43
Needing to reauthor the story of my life	
LIFE-GIVING THINGS	44
Steaming hot showers on freezing cold mornings	
ENLIGHTENED	46
Like rays of sunshine	

ABOUT THE AUTHOR

Kim P. Sami grew up in south-western Sydney, Australia.

Her literary career commenced as a primary student with the publication of her first poem, *Birds* in Sydney's *Sunday Telegraph* newspaper *Charlie Chuckles* section:

> Up, up, up in the sky,
> see the birds flying high
> Soaring down among the trees,
> their colourful feathers are sure to please
> Birdwatchers sitting quietly below,
> wishing the birds would stay still, but no!
> They must be on their merry way,
> no matter what the time of day.

While a keen reader and English student, Kim also enjoyed Mathematics, and journalling. She completed her Bachelor of Science degree through the University of Sydney, graduating in 1986.

Kim worked as a superannuation consultant for three years before being retrenched, returning to university, and completing her Social Work degree in 1996. It was here that she started writing poetry while reflecting on life. This practice continues to the present day.

After attending a symposium about writing and publishing, Kim decided to take her writing more seriously. She became a member and is the current secretary of her local Fellowship of Australian Writers' group (FAW) and commenced sending her poetry to different writing publications. Kim's first success, *The Knowing Gums,* was published in Ariel Chart, in April 2020:
http://www.arielchart.com/2020/04/the-knowing-gums.html?m=1

After competing in the Half-Marathon of The Poetry Marathon 2020 online, one of her poems, *The Light Giver*, was accepted for publication in the *2020 Poetry Marathon Anthology* .

Kim is a singer, a person of faith, loves people, reading most genres, handicrafts, her NRL team St George Illawarra, and travel. She lives with her husband and two dogs in the Macarthur region of Sydney, Australia.

Contact the author at:
E: kimpsami@gmail.com
W: www.kimpsami.com.au
M: PO Box 4235
         Bradbury NSW 2560

Author photograph by David Amos
Contact David at:
davidamosphotography@gmail.com

ACKNOWLEDGEMENTS

My first thank you has to be to Mauro Di Nicola, for his continued commitment, encouragement and support of me personally and of my writing ability, over all these years. Mauro, thank you for seeing so much more in the shy, serious 16-year-old I was than I could see in myself, far beyond my potential to publish. I have no words to describe the profound impact you have had, and continue to have, in my life.

Thank you to Trish Watts and her use of Voice Movement Therapy, which was just what I needed at an extremely stressful and transitional time of my life. So many of these poems came out of my reflections on our sessions. Trish, you've given me the courage to listen to the Spirit and dare to truly live the life of abundance that Jesus promises.

Many thanks to our President, Victoria Chie, my writing buddy, Miriam Skerra, and all the members of our Fellowship of Australian Writers (F.A.W.) Macarthur Branch who, from the moment I arrived for my first meeting around 3 years ago, made me not only feel welcome, but have encouraged me with their respectful and constructive suggestions, be it poetry or short stories. Thank you for creating such a safe space to explore and expand my craft.

To Maureen Kelly, Honorary NSW Secretary (F.A.W), who provided me with valuable contacts and assistance in finding the right people and resources needed to start on this self-publishing journey, thank you and many hugs. I hope to see you in our neck of the woods when borders re-open. You are always welcome!

To Jo Forestier, Canberra F.A.W., who gave me valuable information on her own self-publishing journey and for introducing me to Barbie, so this book could be born.

To Barbie Robinson, for her invaluable assistance in the whole production process, generously sharing the wealth of her experience with me, a complete novice in the self-publishing realm. Thank you for your patience, dedication, responsiveness and care in helping me to bring my dream to fruition. I could not have done this without you.

To Dee Copeland, my illustrator, whose skill, and prayerful artwork has added so much to my words. Thank you, Dee. Here's to many more collaborative projects and a lifetime of friendship.

Thank you to my husband, Augustine, for his continued love and support in everything I do. I love you.

For the Spirit of Life within me who has never let me go, I offer my humble thanks and praise.

To all of you, and for the many others who have been companions on my life's journey to this point: 'I thank my God each time I think of you, and when I pray for you, I pray with joy.' (*I Thank my God*, hymn by Frank Anderson M.S.C)

www.ingramcontent.com/pod-product-compliance
Lightning Source LLC
Chambersburg PA
CBHW060530010526
44110CB00052B/2555